# GOVERNMENT REGULATION: WHERE DO WE GO FROM HERE?

John Charles Daly, *Moderator*

John C. Danforth
Paul W. MacAvoy
William Proxmire
Harrison Wellford



A Round Table held on December 19, 1977
and sponsored by
the American Enterprise Institute for
Public Policy Research
Washington, D.C.

This pamphlet contains the edited transcript of
one of a series of AEI forums.
These forums offer a medium for
informal exchanges of ideas on current policy problems
of national and international import.
As part of AEI's program of providing opportunities
for the presentation of competing views,
they serve to enhance the prospect
that decisions within our democracy will be based
on a more informed public opinion.
AEI forums are also available on
audio and color-video cassettes.

AEI Forum 14



ISBN 0-8447-2121-2
Library of Congress Catalog Card No. 78-51420
*Printed in United States of America*

JOHN CHARLES DALY, former ABC news chief and forum moderator: This public policy forum, part of a series presented by the American Enterprise Institute, deals with the subject of government regulation: Where do we go from here?

We might begin this discussion with a brief history of government regulation. Regulation probably began in 1789, when a government agency was established to regulate the duties collected on imported goods. In that same year, President Washington established another federal agency to regulate the payment of pension benefits to Revolutionary War veterans.

Acronyms began to be used in 1887, with the establishment of the Interstate Commerce Commission (ICC). In 1906, the Food and Drug Act produced a regulatory agency to protect public health. The Great Depression produced the Civil Aeronautics Board, the Federal Communications Commission, the Federal Maritime Commission, the Federal Power Commission, the Securities and Exchange Commission, and so forth.

In the 1960s, regulation took a new turn, seeking primarily to meet social objectives rather than economic needs. Thus, the Equal Employment Opportunity Commission, the Occupational Safety and Health Administration, the Environmental Protection Agency, the Consumer Product Safety Commission, and other such agencies were created.

After almost two hundred years of effort, we have

created a labyrinth of regulatory agencies that affect every aspect of American life. Paradoxically, major criticisms of the complexity and authority of the regulatory labyrinth were first voiced during its golden hours, the New Deal. At that time, President Franklin Roosevelt established the President's Committee on Administrative Management (the Brownlow Committee), the report of which concludes that the independent regulatory commissions constitute a serious and increasing problem.

The report stated that they obstruct effective overall management in the executive branch of the government and hinder coordination of policy. Two Hoover Commissions studied the organization of the executive branch under Presidents Truman and Eisenhower, and President Kennedy, prior to his inauguration, commissioned James M. Landis to report on the regulatory agencies.

In 1964, President Johnson established the Administrative Conference of the United States to reform the regulatory process, and President Nixon established the President's Advisory Council on Executive Organization (the Ash Council) in 1969.

President Ford and the Congress took measures toward reform in several areas, and President Carter made regulatory reform a major issue in his presidential campaign.

Yet, the way out of the regulatory labyrinth still eludes us, and the question remains, where do we go from here?

Senator Proxmire, does the present Congress consider government regulation a serious problem? If so, is the problem getting sufficient attention?

William Proxmire, United States senator (Democrat, Wisconsin): Yes, Congress does recognize that regulation is a serious problem, and the conflicting attitudes by congressmen toward the problem reflect the differing concerns of their constituents.

First, Congress and the public realize that one of the

great concerns of our society in the last ten to twenty years has been environmental protection, and this concern has been reflected in constructive legislation. Congress has also attempted to deal with the deep public concern about protecting safety and health, and that's very constructive.

At the same time, there is a conflicting view that there is just too much government. Not only are taxes too high, but also government is seen as interfering too much in the areas of environmental protection and safety and health. So, we have a real conflict.

Also, people look to the government and regulations to solve the very serious problem of inflation. They think that regulation, if handled properly, can ease the great burden of rising prices.

Thus, these conflicting concerns of the public are reflected in the Congress, which will take constructive action, in this year and in coming years, in addressing them.

MR. DALY: Senator Danforth, can the present regulatory structure be made to operate more effectively, or is a completely new structure necessary?

JOHN C. DANFORTH, United States senator (Republican, Missouri): It is not enough just to tinker with the existing system, although it is worthwhile to comb through all of the existing regulations and try to eliminate those that are useless or unduly burdensome.

I am beginning to think, though, that we need to approach the problem on a more structural and systematic basis. We should not just look at those regulations which are particularly damaging, but should determine which general areas are appropriate for regulation and which are not. We must think of alternatives to the rigid regulatory structure that we now have, and perhaps we should set general performance goals and offer a system of rewards or penalties depending on whether or not those goals are met. At present, we merely zero in on particular regulations and try to solve every problem by simply putting out a new book of regulations.

MR. DALY: Dr. Wellford, you headed President Carter's transition team on government reorganization. What is the administration's approach to reform?

HARRISON WELLFORD, executive associate director for reorganization and management, Office of Management and Budget: I agree with Senator Danforth that it is very important to determine the appropriate scope of federal intervention in the private sector. We feel that federal regulation of the transportation industry has been excessive. Therefore, the administration will emphasize increased competition in the transportation area.

We are entering a new era of regulatory policy with this administration. The last decade was characterized by major legislation that extended the reach of regulation into vast new areas. While the increased protection from occupational, environmental, and consumer regulation has brought great benefits, we should recognize that some of these new programs were introduced in response to crises, and that the result was hasty legislation and hasty regulation.

As a result, we have a system in which emphasis on regulatory goals and a relative lack of attention to good management have resulted in delay, overlap, conflict between regulations, and unnecessary burdens on the private sector.

So, in addition to transportation deregulation, the administration is emphasizing improvements in the management of the entire regulatory process.

MR. DALY: In your judgment, Professor MacAvoy, what is

the net impact of government regulation on the overall economy?

Paul W. MacAvoy, professor of economics, Yale University, and AEI adjunct scholar: Mr. Daly, there are as many economists' views as to what regulation does as there are regulatory commissions. The problem is to summarize these views in some way that indicates an overall effect from the behavior of the commissioners.

Some of my colleagues may not agree with me, but I believe that the effect of regulation has been to increase the prices consumers pay for goods and services. For instance, trucking rates are too high, and airline rates are $5 or $6 billion a year too high. As a result of regulations by the Federal Energy Administration and the Federal Power Commission, energy prices, too, may be $5 or $6 billion too high. Until recently, the FEA required 600,000 reports to be submitted every year by companies that produce energy. The cost of filling out these reports adds $150 to $200 million to our household bills.

It is more difficult to generalize in the case of health and safety regulation. It appears from gross national product accounts that environmental regulation, which is Senator Proxmire's concern and mine, does add a few points to the Consumer Price Index, and that safety regulation requires investment in equipment that adds ultimately to the cost to consumers.

Economists seem to believe that regulation has begun, finally, to affect the overall performance of the economy, which used to grow at around 4 percent per year. It now looks as if a percentage point or more of that growth has been sacrificed to regulatory activities. Thus, over a ten- to twenty-year period, economic growth will be significantly less than it would have been in the absence of these regulations.

It is difficult to measure the effect on growth, but it

appears that the cost in reduced growth rate is not compensated for by the benefits in workplace safety, or environmental quality, or by better airline or trucking service.

SENATOR PROXMIRE: But the way we measure GNP is very unsatisfactory. Senator Fulbright was always frustrated with the gross national product; the more that is wasted, in some ways, the greater the GNP. The gross national product does not necessarily measure quality or achievement of any particular kind. It just adds up all of the goods and services, some of which may be counterproductive.

PROFESSOR MACAVOY: Of course.

SENATOR PROXMIRE: So, when we require a company to build equipment to protect the environment at a cost of $15 or $20 million, that is reflected as growth in the GNP.

It seems to me that we must develop some kind of economic impact requirement for environmental action in order to have some clear notion of the cost of environmental protection. In many cases, this would move us in the direction of getting a greater quality in our GNP.

PROFESSOR MACAVOY: It would accomplish even more than that, Senator Proxmire, in that we could begin to measure the benefits that flow from these health and safety regulatory activities.

The first step we must take is to look at changes that have occurred in the physical dimensions of safety or environmental quality. For example, what has happened to accident rates as a result of regulations by our infamous OSHA? What has happened to particulate matter in the atmosphere as a result of EPA enforcement? What has happened to the number of accidents in the household, as a result of Consumer Product Safety Commission activity?

The figures, crude though they may be, show no significant impact as a result of all this regulatory activity. By creating the Great Recession of 1975, the Council of Economic Advisers did more to reduce particulate matter in the atmosphere than EPA did in its lifetime. [Laughter.]

SENATOR PROXMIRE: Isn't it true, though, that in 1976 for the first time in history, we had cleaner air than we had the previous year, in spite of the growth in the economy and the growth in industrial activity?

PROFESSOR MACAVOY: During the first half of 1976, we had a deep recession, which had a greater effect on stack emission reduction than various pieces of EPA required plant and equipment.

The only area in which we have had some reduction in emissions is the automotive area, because Congress set standards which could not be changed through the administrative process. In other areas, we have not been effective in reducing whatever we are trying to reduce. At the same time, there has been a great deal of investment, because industry must meet equipment standards.

We have the worst of both worlds; we have equipment that does very little and costs a great deal, which is what the administrator requires, and we have the case-by-case exceptions which dilute environmental efforts.

SENATOR DANFORTH: We have pursued the wrong goal in many of these regulations. We have not focused on the results that we want to accomplish. Instead, we have focused on the means by which regulators think goals should be accomplished. Instead of determining how many man-days are lost in an industry as a result of accidents in the workplace, we are deciding such matters as how big is a hole, and when is a ceiling a floor, and how high should the fire extinguisher be from the floor, and so forth.

We have unleashed an army of inspectors, who move

through the country, not for the sake of creating safer job sites, but for the sake of enforcing regulations which were believed by the regulators to create safer job sites. We need to put less emphasis on the regulator's conception of appropriate safety or pollution measures, and focus instead on the result we want to achieve.

If we seek to reduce the number of man-days lost in an industry, then we should set a goal-oriented standard, providing rewards in the form of tax incentives for meeting the standard and penalties for not meeting it. Let's leave it to the industry that is being regulated to determine the means of accomplishing the goal, rather than have the regulator determine the means and then police the industry.

DR. WELLFORD: The question of how to measure the benefits of regulation is a fascinating one, and one that economists love to debate. We must recognize, though, that in many of the most important regulatory areas it is wrong to expect quantifiable benefits.

I agree with Secretary of Labor Ray Marshall that the design of a toilet seat is not fundamental to the health of the American worker, nor is the number of knotholes in a ladder. But I do think that the absence of carcinogenic vapors and dust in the workplace *is* fundamental. If a hazard is there, and if there is a latency period of twenty years before cancer turns up in the exposed worker, I don't know how we can expect to measure the long-term benefit from reduced exposure today.

The same problems apply in dealing with air pollution, water pollution, and many other areas where long-term hazards, with long latency periods, may occur.

SENATOR PROXMIRE: I wonder if it's that complicated, though. Let me pursue Senator Danforth's proposal, which makes a lot of sense. There is a practical example of how well it has worked in the Ruhr River in Germany. That river is the most intensely used by industry in the world. Almost every kind of polluter is on it—coal, steel, chemical companies, and so forth. Yet, people sail on it, swim in it, and drink it. Why? Because there is exactly the kind of incentive system that Senator Danforth proposes. It makes sense.

The industries on the Ruhr River have to pay a tax, depending on the amount of pollution they put into the river. In other words, they recognize that water is no longer a free good; it is an economic good.

Industries know that they can maximize their profits by reducing the amount of pollution they put into the river. It is true that there are limits on this, and that it is not always easy to measure, but it is an objective system that has gotten good results. We should move in that direction. I favor it, and have introduced a bill to do it. Incidentally, I think this panel should discuss regulation of the banking industry, because it is an area that the Carter administration needs to work on.

Mr. Daly: If there is no objection, we will move into a new area, banking. Go ahead, Senator Proxmire.

Senator Proxmire: When President Carter was running for office, one of his campaign promises was to simplify government organization. He talked about reducing the number of agencies in Washington to 200 and so forth.

In banking, we have an opportunity that begs for the Carter solution. We have three separate agencies to regulate banking, and the result is much duplication and waste. In the words of the venerable Arthur Burns, this is "a competition in laxity," and we do not have the kind of regulation for banking that we ought to have.

Now, I am delighted to say that in December 1977, the Government Affairs Committee staff reported a bill which supports unifying these agencies, so that, at long last, we will have the kind of orderly regulation of banking we ought to have.

This bill will require support from the administration, because—no question about it—we will continue to get opposition from the American Bankers Association, which likes to have permissive regulators.

We are also opposed by the bureaucracy, which likes to preserve its empire, and the only way we will get this legislation through is by getting some support from you, Dr. Wellford, in the Office of Management and Budget, previously headed by Bert Lance, an eminent banker who didn't like this idea. [Laughter.]

Dr. Wellford: I am delighted to be able to discuss this issue with my Democratic colleague. [Laughter.]

We have looked at the draft of the report put out by Senator Ribicoff's committee, and we have had staff looking at the banking regulatory area for some time.

Given the fact that the present climate in Congress makes it difficult to pass a bill for the widows and orphans of senators, let alone substantive legislation, we have had to choose our priorities for the next year very carefully. [Laughter.]

I mentioned earlier that we have decided to increase competition in the transportation area. We will emphasize this in 1978. We have put a lot of support behind the airline deregulation bill this year. Next we intend to address proposals for increasing competition in the trucking industry. When those two tasks have been accomplished, we will be able to turn to other areas, including banking. But, at the present time, it is hard to argue that anything is more important than addressing the transportation area.

Senator Proxmire: We are not asking that you say this banking bill is first on your priority agenda. We just want the administration to announce its support. Secretary Blumenthal has said he does not want to do that. Of course, the comptroller of the currency is under his jurisdiction—and therefore the bill would cut down on his empire. [Laughter.]

We just want the President to say he favors the bill. We will take it from there—or try to.

PROFESSOR MACAVOY: A cry from the right for diversity, Senator. A great deal of reform has already taken place in regulation of financial institutions, insurance companies in particular. In Massachusetts, we now have accounts that will allow us to earn interest on checking deposits, and the banks have not failed as a result. Banks in Massachusetts fail occasionally, but the overall effect there has been to distribute income substantially in favor of consumers. That would never have happened if the Federal Reserve were setting standards for interest rates on checking deposits.

SENATOR PROXMIRE: But Massachusetts has Carol Greenwald, a marvelous commissioner that neither a Republican nor a Democratic administration would appoint to anything because she vigorously defends the public interest. What Carol Greenwald did in regulating the banks there has been great, and we should have that kind of diversity. But how much diversity do you want?

We do not need three separate federal regulators, in addition to the fifty state regulators, all trying to do the same thing in the same industry. Banking is the only industry in that category, and I submit that regulation of our financial institutions lags far behind regulation in the other areas where there is a unified regulator.

PROFESSOR MACAVOY: MacAvoy's Massachusetts law—Competition among regulators drives out excess regulation. [Laughter.]

SENATOR PROXMIRE: Whoever believes that will believe anything.

SENATOR DANFORTH: I think that Professor MacAvoy has made a good point about diversity, and I share his point of view.

SENATOR PROXMIRE: Do you want three Federal Power Commissions?

SENATOR DANFORTH: No. I was referring to the relationship between state governments and the federal government. Take the Community Development program, for example. Not long ago, I met with mayors from a number of communities in St. Louis County in my state, who told me that the Community Development program has gone sour, and that they have become inundated with regulations.

In St. Anne, a suburb of St. Louis, in order to compete for $62,000 of Community Development money, they have had to hire a full-time employee just to process the forms that are required.

What was originally conceived as a block grant program, designed to permit more diversity and more decision making throughout the country, has somehow become perverted. Secretary Harris's position, as I understand it, is that we really don't want all those decisions to be made out there. We want to put more strings on the way in which federal funds are spent by the rest of the country.

Thus, we have developed more forms, more restrictions, and more regulation. And maybe the whole problem of regulation, or at least a good part of it, is the pretentiousness that we, in Washington, have; the notion that somehow this is the font of all wisdom, and that if only we can make the decisions, we will make the right decisions.

If we allow people to make decisions in the marketplace, as to how to make a product safer or how to pollute less, or if we allow the city of St. Anne, Missouri, to decide how it will spend its Community Development money, we feel that somehow they will foul it up. Therefore, we aggregate this responsibility to ourselves.

I believe that this philosophical problem underlies the whole problem of regulation.

SENATOR PROXMIRE: But, Senator, you are talking about federal money. Community Development money doesn't come from the states; it comes from the federal government.

If the federal government supplies the funds, then it is the government's duty to the taxpayers to make sure the money is spent properly.

SENATOR DANFORTH: But how can we know the proper way to spend it?

SENATOR PROXMIRE: Let me tell you how it was spent before. The National Association of Housing and Redevelopment officials found that in 1975 more Community Development money was spent in high-income census tracts than in low-income census tracts.

The law says this money is to be spent for low- and moderate-income people. So, Secretary Harris is right to insist that when federal money is involved, it must be spent for low-income people, as the law intends.

SENATOR DANFORTH: The Community Development program does that, and so does the Law Enforcement Assistance program.

SENATOR PROXMIRE: Do you want them to build tennis courts?

SENATOR DANFORTH: We are using federal funds properly in

assisting universities and hospitals. We even went so far as to give grants to medical schools on the condition that they admit people from foreign medical schools.

The real question is, Who is making the decisions in this country? We have used the leverage of the federal dollar to say to local communities, state governments, and universities that we will reserve the right to make all the important decisions. Particularly in the case of matching fund requirements, we have really twisted around an important tradition of our country, that of local self-government.

SENATOR PROXMIRE: The best answer, of course, is to just stop spending the money. If you want to advocate that, I'll go along with you. [Laughter.]

DR. WELLFORD: I am fascinated by what has been said, and I'll take issue with part of it. The federal government has created a red-tape jungle in trying to direct how its money is to be spent at the local level. The administration has just completed a review of all of the planning required by the federal government when it makes an economic assistance program available to state and local governments. We have forced every agency that imposes a planning requirement to consider several points: Is it really necessary? Can we standardize it? Is it in conflict with another planning requirement?

All the results are not in, but I think we will bring about a substantial reduction in the paperwork required for federal programs. There is a vast consulting industry now, whose primary business is to help state and local jurisdictions fill out forms so they can get federal money.

But there is another aspect to the problem. First, many of these planning requirements are mandated by Congress, and only Congress can change them. Second, the whole area of economic assistance, the $50 billion that we're spending in urban areas, for example, is honeycombed with single-purpose programs without any real coherence or strategy to direct them. The fundamental questions that must be addressed are: What purpose are all these programs serving? What is the target we want to hit? And, what kind of federal organization is best suited to pursuing that target? Since Congress has been largely responsible for creating this problem, it must also help to find the solution.

MR. DALY: The last formal comprehensive review of problems in the regulatory area was made by the Domestic Council Review Group established by President Ford in 1974, which submitted its report in January 1977.

According to that report, conventional wisdom held that most of the holes, that most of the shortcomings in regulation result from unqualified personnel, cumbersome organizational structure, or inefficient operating procedures. The council agreed that reforms were needed in these management areas, but it believed that the basic trouble lay deeper.

The report added that some regulation just does not make sense—and it gave the CAB as an example—and that in areas where federal intervention is needed, it has been ineffective, or inefficient, because the agencies have not been using appropriate tools. Here, the example was OSHA. The report also said that far greater efforts were needed to determine the social and economic effects of regulation.

The thrust of the report is that a vast amount of information exists. Around $500 million a year are spent on statistical and other research data, yet this information is not gathered efficiently in a central location to provide for sensible decision making.

SENATOR PROXMIRE: There is a lot of truth in that. In my view, the solution is to recognize that some regulator cies can be abolished. For example, I favor just abolishing the Interstate Commerce Commission.

President Ford took a constructive step in that direction by proposing to greatly reduce the ICC's tendency to do precisely the opposite of what it was created to do in 1887. It was created to hold down the railroad rates for the farmers at a time when railroads were the only method of transportation. There is enormous potential competition in transportation now, but the ICC holds the rates up. That is why I think some of these agencies should be abolished.

Other agencies can rely on disclosure as the principal means of regulation. What, after all, is the most effective regulatory body we have in Washington? In my view, it is the Securities and Exchange Commission, which does a superb job.

Today's paper was filled, as usual, with attacks on controversial SEC decisions, but I think almost everybody approves the vigorous, honest, and effective way the agency operates. The SEC is effective because it relies on disclosure.

The other thing we should rely on more is antitrust action, recognizing that competition is the principal regulatory element in our society.

SENATOR DANFORTH: I completely agree with the emphasis on antitrust. That is one very promising substitute for all this regulation—to allow a competitive marketplace to regulate itself. The greatest opponents of deregulation are the industries that are regulated. They really don't want the competition. For example, when the airline bill was under discussion, the Commerce Committee hearing room was filled with representatives of the airlines who were opposed to deregulation; they wanted to keep the present system.

MR. DALY: It was not unanimous, though.

SENATOR DANFORTH: It was not unanimous, but many were

opposed to deregulation. The same is true in trucking. When I was attorney general of Missouri, we had a Board of Embalmers. Now, what is the public interest in regulating embalming? As far as the public is concerned, what difference does it make? It's too late. [Laughter.]

But the embalmers saw it as a way to limit competition in the industry.

Senator Proxmire: That's an excellent point. The people who are being regulated are often the ones who want it that way.

In the area of electronic media regulation, there is the crudest kind of interference with the First Amendment rights of radio and television. After all, 74 percent of the people get their principal news on radio and television. Yet, the stations are subject to censorship, and their licenses have been cancelled under some circumstances. At one time or another, the Johnson, Nixon, and Kennedy administrations all interfered with radio and television in clear violation of the First Amendment.

It seems to me that we should allow the FCC to do no more than prevent engineering interference with the various frequencies. We should simply let the highest bidder secure a radio or television station and allow him to operate with the same immunity that printed media has.

Professor MacAvoy: We agree widely on what should be done, Senator Proxmire, but there is real confusion among economists about how to do it. A professor in South Carolina took your suggestion of abolishing the ICC seriously and looked into the possibility of tearing the building down and then salting the earth so nothing would grow there ever again, and found that he couldn't get an environmental impact statement—[Laughter.]

But seriously, the question is, How can we get ICC reform through Congress? The ICC has been a subject of trenchant criticism by Presidents Kennedy, Johnson, Nixon, and Ford. And now, with Dr. Wellford's help, Mr. Carter is beginning to criticize it as well.

One approach would be to take the bill back for revision to a subcommittee of the Senate Commerce Committee for review by the individuals who wrote the original bill, perhaps four or five senators who were there in 1887. [Laughter.] What's wrong with that is that many members of Congress do not take kindly to the notion that the Act to Regulate Commerce is no longer exactly right. They take testimony from those in the industry who insist that there will be utter chaos and disruption if this bill is passed. And then economists from the administration enter the debate, and representatives of industry demand proof from the economists that there will be no chaos in the market as a result of reform. The proposition that those who reform must bear the burden of predicting everything that will happen in the future makes reform impossible. How can we change Congress, Senator, to put the burden of proof on those who are now advantaged by the special-interest regulation?

SENATOR PROXMIRE: Unfortunately, it is very difficult to reduce or modify regulation.

But we must grasp our opportunities. That is why we have such a marvelous opportunity to reform the banking industry. [Laughter.]

Thanks to Bert Lance, to the problem banks, and to the fact that we have had many bank failures recently, this is the time to act. And if we can get the administration to support us, we can probably get it through. [Laughter.]

MR. DALY: We're going to start charging you by the minute, Senator. [Laughter.]

Let us come back to an important point. The report of the Domestic Council Review Group said that, in the regulatory area, almost without exception, policy has been formulated in unnecessary ignorance. Decisions have been made on the basis of guesses or flimsily held beliefs with very little attention to the actual economic or social consequences of regulation. Clearly, the report recommends that we do a better job of getting information before we legislate.

Do you think that is reasonable, Senator Danforth?

SENATOR DANFORTH: Yes, I think that is absolutely right. I have been in Congress for only a year, and I am amazed at how much business is done on the backs of envelopes.

The public demands safe jobs. It demands clean air and clean water. Therefore, when a bill comes before Congress, the congressmen, who are politicians, do not want to appear to be against safety on the job, so they vote for the legislation without really understanding what its effects will be.

It is important to understand that we in the Congress are not a bunch of wizards.

PROFESSOR MACAVOY: But the problems of obtaining information to make a complex decision on the appropriate level of electric power prices in Wisconsin or Massachusetts, for example, are immense. And the agencies working to make a regulatory decision take too long. They generate vast piles of data and can only *approximate* price levels. Because of the high inflation rates and low economic growth rates of the last few years, many of those approximations have been wrong. Thus, the system is generating biased data which do not work well but rather set prices which cut off investment.

The consensus among economists is that there are certain things regulatory agencies try to do that they never can do. One of these things is using price regulation of public utilities as a substitute for an income tax system. Mr. Carter's energy plan, which is now before Congress, is motivated by the notion that the oil companies must be prevented from making excess profits. And in order to ensure that, we will have to set prices. The notion that price controls are a good way of reducing profits and would substitute well for the tax system is fundamentally defective. What the controls do is substitute for a competitive market. That kind of substitute for a tax system generates very high costs and inefficiencies in competitive markets.

SENATOR PROXMIRE: I disagree with the implications of your statement and with Senator Danforth's notion that everything is done on the backs of envelopes.

I suppose that is true to a certain extent, but the fact is we have a terrific system for eliciting information and data. Sometimes we don't use it as much as we should, but the information is there.

The real problem is power. When we attempt to make needed changes, the people who oppose us make campaign contributions to enough congressmen to defeat us. Or opponents of reform can organize sufficient interest among labor union members and others so that they have an intense feeling on that one issue. It may be only 3 or 4 percent of the constituency, but that is enough to swing a close election.

That is the kind of situation that we have to overcome. And it can be overcome if the President of the United States uses his prestige, and if we try to mobilize and organize these arguments as well as we can.

DR. WELLFORD: We recently issued a proposed executive order that attempts to address that problem. The basic purpose of the executive order is to bring major regulatory options to public attention and to government attention much earlier.

Traditionally, the public first learns about a regulatory initiative, and one regulatory agency learns about an initiative by another, when a notice of proposed rule making is put in the *Federal Register.* We have proposed that a regulatory agenda be created much earlier in the process, before a final proposal has been made within an agency. It might even be announced in the *Federal Register*.

This would encourage a much more rigorous exploration of alternatives to a particular regulatory action, and would help us to discover whether or not the agency has chosen the most effective, least burdensome way of getting a particular job done.

Something like that, an economic analysis of regulatory impact, was tried in the Ford administration. But the problem with that process was that it came too late in the game. We want to consider alternatives earlier, so there can be a much fuller debate.

PROFESSOR MACAVOY: The problem with our process is that no agency ever wrote an economic impact statement showing that the impact of its rule making was adverse. [Laughter.]

MR. DALY: There is one more area that we should cover. In 1974, President Ford sent a reform program to the Congress, one element of which was that Congress should establish a national commission on regulatory reform to report on unnecessary and costly rules and practices of ten independent regulatory agencies.

The Senate Government Affairs Committee held some hearings, but soon the program died. Now we have the Ribicoff-Percy-Byrd bill before the Congress, which requires that the President submit a comprehensive reform proposal for at least one segment of American industry. Then the transportation industry, for example, or the financial institutions, and Congress would have a certain number of months to consider it. If they took no action, the President's proposals would become the first item on the calendar. Isn't it true that the Congress and the executive branch would benefit from working together in this way?

SENATOR PROXMIRE: I like that bill very much. I certainly would vote for it. It would force us to take some kind of action by a particular time. We have talked and talked about regulatory reform, but have not made progress. This would compel us to focus on some kind of reform measures.

I think that consideration of financial institutions ought to precede consideration of transportation, of course, but—[Laughter.]

MR. DALY: It is time now to let our distinguished friends in the audience open the question-and-answer session. May I have the first question, please?

FRANK GRAD, professor of law, Columbia Law School: I have the impression that a great deal of the discussion relating to regulatory reform really stems from dissatisfaction with the quality of life itself. Life was much simpler without OSHA, without EPA, without any number of the hazards that we are regulating.

In many instances, people are opposed, not just to the complexity of the regulations, but to the regulatory process itself. This reflects public dissatisfaction with the kind of life we are leading.

Would the senators comment on this?

SENATOR DANFORTH: There is a lot to be said for that point of view. Many people feel that they have lost control over their destinies, that their own lives are not theirs to live, and that they are being ordered about for no particular purpose. Many people complain about the amount of red tape, and people in business complain that regulations change all the time, that they are not predictable.

Throughout the country, people sense that, instead of being able to make decisions for themselves, they are being batted back and forth on some irrational basis by faceless bureaucrats who make the decisions for them.

SENATOR PROXMIRE: I agree. Naturally, people would like to live a simpler life and reflect back on what seemed to be happier times before technology brought about sweeping changes and complications. But a relatively small number of people think this way. Many of them are the environmental enthusiasts, in favor of preserving the wilderness and establishing environmental protections. By and large, though, I don't think this is a major concern.

PROFESSOR MACAVOY: OSHA provided the most poignant example of this phenomenon.

We tried last year to read and comprehend a set of OSHA physical standards relating to the guarding equipment that goes on machinery. These standards were given in the regulations in the form of appliqués on design drawings of equipment. OSHA enforcement officers go into machine shops with these standards in hand and say, for instance, that the piece of plastic guarding the moving part is a quarter of an inch too far from the moving part.

We found that there are approximately twenty-five generic types of equipment, and, in the regulations, there were exquisitely detailed design drawings of about eight types. The machines were of 1930 vintage and had long since disappeared, but the regulations contained drawings of safety equipment for them. There was one design drawing which did not have any safety equipment written on it, and it had been included in the regulations by mistake. No one had ever noticed that in the six years of OSHA's lifetime.

Even more interesting, the remaining fifteen or so types of machines have no regulations whatsoever in OSHA standards. There is no OSHA safety standard for a steel rolling mill, and no one had ever noticed it. Most infraction cases seem to have been applied by the enforcement officers on types of machines for which there are no regulations. Factory managers found those infractions so confounding, so detailed, so intricate, that they had no idea that they were being charged with violations of regulations that did not exist.

That's an example of the law getting away entirely from everybody involved, except the enforcement officer, and he wasn't telling. [Laughter.]

Dr. Wellford: OSHA is really a classic agency for demonstrating that point. However, the new head of OSHA, Eula Bingham, has taken steps to remove 1,200 (about 20 percent) of the regulations that her agency has issued, on the grounds that the costs of compliance outweigh any possible benefits from them.

That sort of rigorous, zero-base budgeting approach to regulations on the books is being conducted in many agencies now, and I hope that a more rational system will ultimately result from it.

Professor MacAvoy: I hope she removes those regulations that do not exist from the design drawings.

Dr. Wellford: That makes sense.

Barbara Franklin, commissioner, Consumer Product Safety Commission: I want to pursue this cost-benefit idea a bit further.

As someone who has to make regulatory decisions, I rely on cost-benefit analysis as a framework for decisions. The kinds of questions it forces me to ask provide a very helpful exercise. But I find that the costs are often easier to quantify than the benefits.

We still wrestle with the question of how to value a life saved by one of our regulations. What should we consider as benefits, and how should we go about making quantitative judgments concerning, for instance, the value of a human life?

SENATOR PROXMIRE: I am very interested in the Consumer Product Safety Commission, which has come before the Appropriations subcommittee of which I am chairman.

The Consumer Product Safety Commission has improved greatly in recent years, but it still has a long way to go because it did not establish its priorities in the beginning.

The basis of judgment should be the number of lives now lost that might be saved if products are improved, and the number of serious injuries that might be prevented.

As a classic example, one of the first products the Consumer Product Safety Commission chose to study was the swimming pool slide. It found, after considerable time was spent in designing standards for the slides, that adults, not children, were most often injured on them, because they would slide into empty swimming pools when they had been imbibing spirits rather freely. [Laughter.]

SENATOR DANFORTH: The commission's objective should be to focus on the ultimate goal of saving lives and preventing injuries, and to determine what kind of reward or penalty is necessary to induce industries to attain a certain measure of safety in their products.

In setting up a standard of safety, we should determine how many lives are now lost, and how many could be saved, how many injuries are now incurred, and how many could be prevented by safe practices. Then we must determine what kinds of economic incentives are necessary to put weight behind that kind of practical judgment.

That kind of determination is often not made. Instead of emphasizing sensible safety measures, we too often focus on what kinds of regulations make sense to the regulators and on the enforcement of those regulations.

So, the cost-benefit analysis is not an analysis of the ultimate objective, but an analysis of the regulation itself.

PROFESSOR MACAVOY: The senator is on a line of inquiry that economists and technicians deeply appreciate. If we can avoid having to make an artificial estimate of the value of a human life, by putting data in the computer and getting garbage out because it depends upon twelve assumptions, by all means, let's do so. In many instances, the issue is not whether some policy is necessary or justifiable, but that, of twelve different ways to save lives, which costs the least?

That issue has come up with respect to air bags, safety belts, and other devices in automobiles. We cannot determine the value of a human life saved by the air bag, but we can determine whether or not accidents could be reduced by some other method that does not impose a $300-per-car cost on consumers.

In a number of instances, we have been able to avoid making these artificial cost-benefit studies, yet we haven't acknowledged that our policy on air bags is a costly way to save a life.

DUANE W. FRIER, Federal Aviation Administration: Senator Proxmire described the congressional system as a terrific system and discussed the need for a greater economic impact assessment of various legislation and administrative actions.

Senator Danforth suggested that there is an administrative warp in the way legislation is being implemented. And he also mentioned that local and state governments are feeling swamped by regulations from the federal bureaucracy. I would like to suggest that within the federal bureaucracy there are many federal bureaucrats who feel that they too are being swamped with too much band-aid type legislation coming at an almost frantic pace from Capitol Hill. The committee process should be able to plug some of the loopholes about which there are complaints. The Appropriations committees can limit the number of people and dollars that the executive branch can devote to implementing legislation, and thereby control it, to some extent. Congress has gotten much larger; it has larger staffs and many more committees. I would like to hear the response of the two senators on the panel to the suggestion that the Congress sit fewer days and consider less legislation.

SENATOR PROXMIRE: Many members of Congress would like that, as would the wives and children of members of Congress, because Congress has been sitting more and more days recently. But the fact is that we have a bigger and more complicated society. The executive branch has grown, our country has grown, and the complexities of our economic system are constantly increasing. I don't know how we can sit fewer days.

It is true that we must establish priorities and deal only with those matters that are important, but it would be a mistake to sit fewer days because we have too much to handle.

That does not necessarily mean we have to pass more laws, or that the laws we pass have to be more comprehensive. But in the future, whether we like it or not, we will have to keep considering the size of the budget. We have a half-trillion dollar budget coming up, and it will continue to grow as time goes on. There is no way to stop that, but we hope we can at least hold back the rate of increase.

Under those circumstances, Congress just has to recognize the need for working longer hours and maintaining larger staffs. I think Mr. Frier has focused on a very important problem, though. I hope we can begin to restrain ourselves to some extent, but I do not think that we can live a simpler life in the future; it is likely to be more complicated.

SENATOR DANFORTH: I have no doubt at all that Congress is, as one newspaper article described it a few years ago, the "bloated" branch of the federal government. It is overstaffed; it meets for too much of the year; and it is busy doing more to the American people than it is doing for the American people.

Staff members are too busy trying to advance their congressman or their senator into some new area that will heighten his prestige. Moreover, we spend too much time issuing press releases about new legislative initiatives and far too little time overseeing the results of the laws we have passed.

HERBERT STEIN, resident scholar, American Enterprise Institute: In this discussion, regulatory reform seems to have been defined as an effort to do something about very old regulatory systems that are entrenched in bureaucracies, congressional committees, and industries, and that look the other way as vast new regulatory plans are imposed.

Might it not be better to pare down our regulatory reform program?

The Carter administration's energy proposals will far exceed in scope many of the regulatory complexities that we talk about reforming. The administration's proposals on regulating the cost of health care, and the steps now being taken to convert the steel industry into a public utility, will also contribute to bureaucratic complexity.

I would like to ask Dr. Wellford if his department in OMB, which is charged with reforming the regulatory process and streamlining the federal government, was consulted in the development of these new regulatory goliaths?

DR. WELLFORD: OMB is consulted on almost everything that happens in the executive branch at some stage. It is my responsibility to comment on the administrative feasibility of some of these regulatory initiatives, and to make sure that alternatives are being considered in the process. We have not been involved in the initiation of the regulations Dr. Stein mentioned.

Professor MacAvoy: Would you care to comment, Dr. Wellford, on the administrative feasibility of having the Federal Energy Regulatory Commission control natural gas well-head prices based upon an index of new oil prices?

Dr. Wellford: We have not seriously analyzed the administrative structure there yet, but let us remember that, until very recently, there was no emphasis whatever on looking at the administrative feasibility of a regulatory initiative, whether it came from Congress or was proposed by the executive branch.

When I took charge of OMB's management branch, in January 1977, it had all the vigor of a sleepy courthouse in south Georgia. It was understaffed and the staff that was there had had very little encouragement in this direction from the leadership of OMB in past administrations. Thus, we do not yet have the capability to do the kind of rigorous analysis that we need to do, but in selective areas we are trying to change that. For example, we need to examine carefully how national health insurance will be administered once the initiative makes it through Capitol Hill.

Senator Proxmire: Let me follow up with a comment on this.

Dr. Stein, after all, has asked something very modest. His question did not imply a drastic cut back in regulation; it implied merely that we should practice some sensible moderation.

He is right that, if we let the steel industry become a public utility, we will be moving in the wrong direction. National health insurance, too, would inevitably create more regulatory problems, more days of sitting in Congress, and more staff. What we must try to do is practice some self-restraint in these areas.

BASIL WHITING, Department of Labor: I am the deputy assistant secretary of that infamous agency, OSHA. [Laughter.]

It's troubled, but workers feel it could and should be an important agency. The fact is that most of the standards about which OSHA is ridiculed were devised by industry on a voluntary basis as guidelines and then were adopted in haste by the preceding administration and given the force of law. That was inappropriate, and we are making a start on improving the situation.

I am troubled, though, by the facile analogy that some cite between environmental regulation and health regulation, and that is the analogy between a pollution tax and a so-called injury tax.

I would like to ask the panel members if they believe there is any justification for an injury tax, in terms of morality and efficiency. My experience suggests that the arguments in favor of an injury tax are quite flawed.

PROFESSOR MACAVOY: We have an injury tax in the form of workers' compensation, which is one of the most comprehensive insurance systems in the country. It provides funds to those who are injured in a factory accident, and thereby makes up for lost wages or income and for the cost of the accident.

These funds eventually derive from payments to an insurance system. The insurance system is faulty in that the amount of the payments a particular factory makes is sometimes not related to its accident rate. If the amount of payments were related to the accident rate, there would be an incentive to reduce accidents in that factory.

If insurance premiums can be adjusted so as to penalize high accident rates, injuries will be kept down even more.

The first step in reform is to make insurance premiums specific with respect to accident rates in each factory. After that occurs, we can deal with questions about particular physical standards on a case-by-case basis. I foresee that, in some instances, there should be outright prohibition of certain kinds of hazards in factories, but if we implement a case-by-case approach, correcting the insurance scheme to penalize high accident rates, we may find we do not need all of those 20,000 OSHA standards.

Dudley H. Chapman, attorney, Washington, D.C.: I see a troubling conflict between the direction of regulatory reform and antitrust. If one is to believe what one reads about the effects of regulatory reform in the securities industry, one of the principal results has been a massive move toward heavy concentration in that industry.

Concentration is, of course, a major bugbear of antitrust, though the Antitrust Division supported that particular reform.

As for Senator Proxmire's idea of abolishing the ICC, one of the major objectives of that legislation was to bring down railroad rates to the farmers, but that was not the only one. The major issue of an earlier time in our nation's history, comparable in its day to Watergate in ours, was the Standard Oil Company. The path to the successful monopoly that John D. Rockefeller built was based on his ability to negotiate more favorable rate reductions from the railroads than his competitors were able to do.

In moving willy-nilly to dismantle the government's regulatory process, will we recreate the same crisis we had in the nineteenth century?

Senator Proxmire: As far as the SEC is concerned, when the fixed commission rates for brokers were abolished and competitive rates were established, it was clear that brokerage firms would be consolidated. We may have only twenty or fewer brokerage firms in the near future, which represents considerable concentration in the industry.

But will that lead to weaker competition or stronger competition? Obviously, there was no competition whatsoever before, because rates were fixed; they were established.

We are beginning to see greater efficiency in the brokerage industry, and investors are getting a better break because the brokerage cost is being reduced. Some of the research that was carried on by the brokerage firms is no longer being done, but I don't think that research was particularly valuable. In general, the SEC has made progress in the area of reform.

As far as the ICC is concerned, my point was that it is an understatement to say we have had a transformation in technology since 1887, especially in transportation technology. We have a highway system and a trucking system that transport a large proportion of our freight. Perhaps abolishing the ICC in a short time would be impossible and a serious mistake. It would have to be phased out gradually, as President Ford proposed. At any rate, it is important to do what we can to provide a real competition among the thousands of individual firms available to compete in trucking. We don't have real competition now. We don't have the access we should have now. We do have deadheading by trucks. We also have an opportunity to reduce the cost of operations and to do something about inflation.

SENATOR DANFORTH: I don't think anyone is suggesting that we move toward deregulation at a breakneck speed. Many industries have been created on the basis of a controlled kind of system. Therefore, if the airline deregulation bill before Congress is passed, it will not cause changes to be made with breakneck speed. The changes will be accomplished over a period of time, so that the businesses involved will have enough time to adjust to the new system.

PROFESSOR MACAVOY: It is important to add that we should try to forecast accurately and thoroughly what is likely to happen to the structure of newly deregulated industries. There were very few proposals to deregulate electric-power price controls, because it was argued that the monopoly at local retail would not produce the quality or quantity of service at the right price for consumers. The notion behind the deregulation of stock commission rates was that, indeed, there would be increased concentration but, as the Senator said so very well, the number of firms would be more vigorously enterprising, even if they were fewer than before.

In the case of the railroads, there has been the advent of trucks, and they have made the reduced number of railroads since 1887 quite a bit more competitive. We had four and a half railroads between Chicago and New York in 1887, and we had a very imperfectly operating cartel that went through a series of rate wars. These conditions do not exist now. Structurally, the industry might be stronger, if it were to reduce its excess capacity the way the stockbrokers have reduced theirs. There could be a phasing process by which we return to a competitive enterprise market for surface transportation.

Economists and lawyers working on these questions have worked very hard on such predictions. They are subject to terrible criticism from the industry for their lack of realism and accuracy. In each case, the issue has been whether we would get an effectively competitive market by reducing regulation. And in each case that I know, the answer seems to be yes, an effectively competitive market does result from reform of regulation. We do not get more monopoly.

DR. WELLFORD: I think you're dead right, the antitrusters and the regulators—or the deregulators, as the case may be—should be talking to each other more.

It's important to mention that in many regulatory initiatives we have developed standards for the larger companies and imposed them on the smaller ones. That has resulted in concentration that is economically unhealthy in the long run. Meat inspection is a classic example. We developed sanitation standards that require expensive technology that may be appropriate for Armour or Swift, but not for a small locker plant in a small town. We have not tried hard enough to make these regulations more flexible, more adaptable to a smaller unit. We have tended to look only at the large successful company, with capital to spend in implementing these regulations, and we have not thought about the small business.

MR. DALY: Next question, please?

HENRY WAKELAND, bureau director, National Transportation Safety Board: I'm speaking only for myself in asking this question. The whole discussion has implied that the effort to raise the safety levels on an economic basis is a matter of trying to raise safety for everyone at once, to benefit everyone. And the only question is whether the benefit is worth the cost.

Now, my observation is that many of the primary reasons for safety regulations derive from a sense of injustice, from a feeling of inequality in seeing one interest group bear the loss for the benefit of an economic gain by another, or in seeing groups at risk who are not protected, who are innocent, who do not know the nature of the hazard before them. OMB regulations have not addressed this question. And I would like to ask whether an administrator is justified in making a safety regulation for the protection of one group against the incursions of another, or for the protection of the innocent who do not know the risks or who are too young or too old.

SENATOR PROXMIRE: Could I ask you to clarify that question?

I'm not sure what you mean by the protection of one group against another when you talk about safety regulation. Can you give us a specific example? Offhand I can't think of any.

Mr. Wakeland: I'll give you an example. Trucks are getting larger, and passenger cars are getting smaller. Passenger cars account for about two-thirds to three-quarters of the fatality loss involving truck transportation in interstate commerce. By not using the latest technology in its safety standards, the trucking industry is making a saving, but the cost is being felt by the other users of the highways.

That is one example. We can find others in other fields.

Senator Proxmire: The example you give certainly does constitute a danger. There are lives lost and a serious number of injuries. There is ample basis for regulations that would require the trucks to use the technology at whatever cost if lives can be saved.

I think Paul MacAvoy has done more work than any of the rest of us have in this area. I'd be curious to know what he thought about it.

Professor MacAvoy: There are problems due to differences of availability of information for different groups of consumers. It may very well be that one group is highly disadvantaged and that we should use a regulatory process not to spread information to them, but to prevent something from occurring to them unduly, if they are more harmed than other groups. Deregulation of automobile insurance accident rates in the beloved state of Massachusetts has impacted certain groups, mostly low-income groups, with very high insurance charges. For political, and maybe economic, reasons, the regulatory reform effort is being reformed to account for this.

But I don't think that argument has much to do with safety regulation. The same argument could be made for regulation of automobile and truck standards if cars were getting larger and trucks were getting smaller. It turns out that recent information may give us an interesting experiment in this area. The findings on the use of safety belts indicate that those who drive foreign cars—Volvo drivers, for example—use belts more frequently and have less injurious accidents. But it also turns out, on further investigation, that they smash pedestrians more often. Now, if you're right, that law should be revised to prevent the use of safety belts in Volvos. [Laughter].

RICHARD HOLMQUIST, American Mining Congress: I'd like to get back to antitrust for just a second. Many industries are faced with worldwide competition, not domestic competition. How do you reconcile our antitrust laws, which are primarily domestically oriented, with worldwide competition? I can cite an example if you like. If we were to break up IBM, Fujitsu would step in and take over the market. How do you reconcile domestic antitrust laws with worldwide competition?

SENATOR DANFORTH: In the context of this program, I'm not sure that we want to get into the international trade question. It opens up whole new vistas.

I just happen to believe that competition has worked pretty well and that we should be expanding and increasing the amount of competition rather than limiting it for the sake of foreign trade. I would rather make sure that our trade is being conducted on a competitive basis and that, for example, the Japanese are not dumping products on the American market. Dumping would be very, very similar to an antitrust violation if it were done domestically.

SENATOR PROXMIRE: The United States has done well in international trade. Of course, right now we are at some disadvantage, but over the years we have done far better than other countries have. We have had a clear antitrust policy as a national policy. It has not been nearly as vigorous as many people would like it to be, or as most of us would like it to be, perhaps. But it has been a policy of supporting competition. I think it tends to promote lower prices and to improve our competitive position, rather than worsen it.

There may be some circumstances where that may not be the case. But I think it is incumbent upon those who can make a special case to make it and to show that there should be some limited exception from the antitrust laws in order to prevent us from losing a serious advantage. The case should be very strong before we permit that exception. By and large, the antitrust laws have served to give us a much more competitive, rather than less competitive, industry.

ROGER NOLL, professor of economics, California Institute of Technology: I'm a member of that special interest group called research scholars who receive grants from the National Science Foundation. And for some surprising reason, my question is to Senator Proxmire. [Laughter.]

On the one hand, as a research scholar in applied economics, there is nothing I would like more than to provide all kinds of information to get the bills passed that Senator Proxmire has sponsored. Most of us regard the idea of reform of the ICC and of banking regulation as a great idea.

On the other hand, in his role as a member of the Appropriations subcommittee that oversees the National Science Foundation, Senator Proxmire has advocated doing away with applied economics research on regulation. He has supported the position that the research might be supported by the agencies themselves, rather than by an independent and less-involved agency. I have two related questions resulting from that.

First, what specific research projects should economists have done in the last two years with that money? I know we are all anxious to do those projects for the senator, if he would just tell us what they are.

And the second question is, what makes you believe that the Interstate Commerce Commission and the Comptroller of the Currency, for example, are more likely to sponsor research on abolishing those agencies than the NSF was? [Laughter.]

SENATOR PROXMIRE: Well, I've given the NSF a few golden fleece awards, but I wasn't aware that I'd given them the golden fleece award in that particular area. I'm glad you called it to my attention. [Laughter.]

I think the National Science Foundation is an excellent agency, and I have supported their budget. I have criticized them in some respects, but after all, I have to do that. They do come before our Appropriations subcommittee. I think the National Science Foundation may very well be the logical agency to make a study of regulation reform. I'm delighted you called this to my attention. If I voted against it, I'll find out why I did. Thank you. [Laughter.]

HENDRIK HOUTHAKKER, Department of Economics, Harvard University: I am glad to hear that both senators present here are in favor of regulatory reform, and that they are aware this means increasing reliance on market forces. My question is a political one. To what extent is this faith in market forces shared by their colleagues in the Senate and in Congress, generally?

SENATOR PROXMIRE: At least the *expressed* faith in the market force is overwhelming. It's hard to find a senator who doesn't express that position. [Laughter.]

Perhaps whether or not they really believe in it can be measured by their votes on various bills. Obviously, this is a very, very troublesome area for congressional action because, as we pointed out, the resistance by the industry being regulated is so strong and so intense. In American politics, the difficulty in getting reform, change, improvement, or progress is that the people who will be affected can be very effective, indeed, in resisting it.

People simply do not forget a vote against their interest. They may agree with a member of Congress on everything else, but if he voted against their interest, that's it—that's the ballgame. And the result is that it is very hard to get that kind of change unless there is an overwhelming consensus that the change should be made, unless other groups will be found who will benefit from the change, unless the President of the United States uses his great influence and prestige and attention to focus interest on it. Only then can it be achieved. But I think that potential for such change is there.

I don't think this is a matter of partisan politics. Virtually all senators would vote for these changes if they could overcome their political problems with the people in their constituencies who strongly resist the changes.

SENATOR DANFORTH: Well, I think it's more than that. The acid test of what members of Congress really believe was the vote on natural gas deregulation, though I hate to keep bringing up the same subject. It is not just a question of what particular interest groups are in favor of airline regulation or truck regulation and the like. Beyond that, there are a very substantial number of members of Congress, maybe a majority, who really believe that we need more regulation, more controls, more cabinet-level departments, and the like.

SENATOR PROXMIRE: Let me just answer that on natural gas deregulation. A few years ago, the cost of natural gas was between 14 and 17 cents per thousand cubic feet. Now it's $1.43 per thousand cubic feet; in the space of about twelve to fifteen years, it has gone up tenfold.

Paul MacAvoy, who is as fine an authority on this as I

know, and a man I deeply admire, said back in 1975 that if the price went to 88 cents per thousand cubic feet, we would have something very close to a balance between supply and demand. Well, the price is now $1.43, and we are still being asked to let the market forces take over. The market forces don't take over—OPEC takes over. The prices rise to the OPEC equivalent price, which may be $2.20, $2.30, or $2.40.

People in Wisconsin—and I think people in Missouri, too—cook with gas, heat with gas, and rely on gas to run their factories. We can understand how they feel when they see the price go through the ceiling with no response in production. There has been no increase in the production of natural gas, and there has been no reduction in consumption. There is no end in sight to these increases. Under these circumstances, regulation makes sense to me.

SENATOR DANFORTH: I can understand that the people in Missouri do, in fact, want natural gas to heat their homes. Although the debate on the subject tends to go on around the clock, the short question is whether one believes in market forces or in expanded governmental controls.

SENATOR PROXMIRE: There are some cases where market forces just don't work, and this is one of them. They have had plenty of opportunities to work, but what has happened? We have had a tenfold increase in price, but have no more production. Do we want a twentyfold increase in price with even less production?

PROFESSOR MACAVOY: There are two lessons in that, Senator. First, you made the mistake of taking MacAvoy's econometric estimates too seriously, and, therefore, you never believed anything that an economist said on the matter after that. [Laughter.]

Second, if what you believe in that case holds, then it

should also hold in regard to sugar and coffee, because the prices of both have gone up as much as natural gas has.

MR. DALY: I think you've both made your point.

This concludes another public policy forum, presented by the American Enterprise Institute for Public Policy Research. On behalf of AEI, our heartfelt thanks to the distinguished and expert panelists, Professor Paul MacAvoy, Senator John Danforth, Senator William Proxmire, and Dr. Harrison Wellford, and our thanks also to our guests and experts in the audience, for their participation. [Applause.]